KNOW THOSE WHO LABOR AMONG YOU!

KNOW THOSE WHO

LABOR AMONG YOU

Sabrina Phillips-Evans

E-mail: evang8sabrina@gmail.com

© 2014

LOWBAR
PUBLISHING COMPANY

905 South Douglas Avenue • Nashville, Tennessee 37204
Phone: 615-972-2842
E-mail: Lowbarpublishingcompany@gmail.com
Web site: www.Lowbarbookstore.com

Edited and Proofed By:
Content Editor: Calvin C. Barlow Jr.
Copy Editor: Lucinda Anderson
Layout Design: James Houston
Cover Design: Tunisa Rice

Unless otherwise indicated, all Scripture quotations are are taken from the King James Version, Amplified Version, and New International Version.

Printed in the United States of America
ISBN 978-0-9886237-2-9
Lowbar Publishing Company
Nashville, Tennessee 37204
615-972-2842
E-mail: Lowbarpublishingcompany@gmail.com

All rights reserved under the International Copyright Law. Contents and /or cover may not be reproduced in whole or in part in any form without the expressed written consent of the author or publisher.

Copyright © 2014

TABLE OF CONTENTS

Acknowledgement

Foreword

Preface *1*

Chapter One
COMMITMENT *11*

Chapter Two
TRUSTWORTHINESS 16

Chapter Three
FAITHFULNESS *19*

Chapter Four
OBEDIENCE *23*

Chapter Five
LOYALTY *25*

Chapter Six
CONCLUSION *27*

ACKNOWLEDGEMENTS

Blessed be our Father, God of all creation and to His Son Jesus the Christ, our Savior and Lord. To the Holy Spirit, our comforter, guide, and teacher.

To my loving husband Glenn, our children, parents, and family members, I am forever grateful for your love and support, which has enabled me to strive beyond my faults and failures to reach goals I once believed were unreachable. Thank you!

I am appreciative of the Christian discipleship of my pastor and the support of my church family. Your prayers have been a great source of strength.

You will fully recognize them by their fruits.

(Matthew 7:16)

FOREWORD

Bishop Calvin C. Barlow Jr., Pastor
Southwest Director of the Home Mission Board
of the National Baptist Convention, USA
Second Missionary Baptist Church
Nashville, Tennessee 37204

As a person who has been involved in the public arena since the age of twelve, I know the importance of valuing other people's contributions. The success or failure of a person's upward mobility is often tied to one's valuing of the thoughts and opinions of other co-workers. We live in a society in which our ability to get along with others is a very important skill set.

Evangelist Sabrina Phillips-Evans, in *Know Those Who Labor among You*, bases her book on years in the public arena as an assistant pastor, proprietor, mother, wife, and office worker. This book does not limit its principles to the private business/public arena, but also speaks to our relationships within the home. It is my personal belief that a myriad of marriages fail due to one partner not placing enough value on the other partner.

The author not only explores the value of co-workers, but looks at our understanding of the positions of co-workers as they relate to the value we assign to the relationship. The author contends that God equips people to work with us in every position in life. This is a practical look that is based on the Scriptures. I recommend this book for every person who seeks harmony in the workplace, whether it is at home, in business, or in the church.

Know Those Who Labor among You is a book that is well worthy of taking the time to read.

Bishop Calvin C. Barlow Jr.

PREFACE

This book was written to bring consciousness to individuals with whom we interact daily, whether it is in our homes, on our jobs, at church, or other familiar places. We must recognize and support those who labor among us. They bring gifts and skills to the table for the purpose of working together in a spirit of agreement and, prayerfully, in a bond of peace. Some are gifted with unique abilities, while others must be trained, but all should be noticed: the serpent as well as the dove (Matthew 10:16). Be wise, my friends!

In the book of Thessalonians, the apostle Paul wrote these words of instruction after receiving a report from Timothy, his son in the faith, concerning the believer's steadfast conviction, "And we beseech you, brethren, to know them which labor among you, and are over you in the Lord, and admonish you." Paul stressed the importance of knowing those workers who toiled faithfully. He went on to say: "I beseech," meaning "to implore" or "I beg," or "plead with you," to take notice, to be aware of, to understand, and to acknowledge." He wanted his readers to respect and appreciate others for their hard work. He said, "For they have refreshed my spirit and yours: therefore, acknowledge them that are such" (1 Corinthians 16:18, KJV).

Working as an administrative assistant in both the secular and Christian arenas has been an interesting learning experience. Finding stability in the roles we play can be difficult at times, because we face many challenges, such as insecurity, jealousness, and ignorance, and sometimes— even sabotage.

It may take a while to sift through personalities, gifts, and talents to see sincerity and hearts with hidden potential. This, however, should not stop you from seeking to know those who labor among you with great admiration. Do not overlook or underestimate the qualities that shape and mold the character of individuals. God equips individuals to work with you in every position and situation. Why else would co-workers put up with our ungodly attitudes and protect our most vulnerable moments? As we learn about and consider others, this experience also prepares us to reach a higher plateau concerning our own destiny, based on our priorities and willingness to be taught. We should proceed confidently in establishing relationships with co-workers with humility of mind and heart.

King Solomon could have requested anything from God: the windows of heaven were open. However, he sought out what was needed to glorify God and to edify the people of God: wisdom to lead and to instruct the children of Israel in the things of God. As Solomon took office, he did not forget his father's teachings, but took on the position of leadership of the Israelites, and became known as the wisest man who ever lived. Therefore, the blessings of God's wealth were also bestowed upon him (see 1 Kings 3:5-15). He honored his position as king, pleased God, and had great compassion towards the people's needs, even above his own. This alone tells us that he had great leadership qualities. Solomon's acceptance of God's leadership and his humility followed the New Testament passage, "Seek ye first the kingdom of God, and His righteousness; and all these things shall be added unto you" (Matthew 6:33, KJV), long before this passage was written. Solomon's priority was seeking the heart and will of God.

When persons of authority realize that God is the giver of all good and perfect gifts, their goals are unlimited and their team workers will support the vision rather than hindering it. It is said that "No man is an island." God is always at work in us. His grace enables us to strive and to become persons of destiny.

Parents often push children to live out their own dreams, when many times children just want to walk in the footsteps of their parents, following the parents' roles. Why do we want our children to be what we are afraid of becoming? What can we do with the days, hours, and minutes available to us so that our mentees can see their possibilities? If you are effectively carrying out your assignment on this earth, in whatever capacity—as employer, parent, pastor, or so forth...know that God has anointed and appointed you for this endeavor. However difficult it may seem—it is worth the challenge, though not just for your own gratification, but also for all those who labor with you. Be strategic in your teaching and in how you train! The leadership qualities you possess move persons away from mediocrity to greatness. There are times when employees will want to take the role of an employer or church members may envision the course of action they would take as if they were the pastor: desire is one thing, but preparation and application are different. It seems like we all can talk a good talk, but meaningful action requires research, studying, writing business plans, and—especially if one is a pastor—spending time with God. If we learn to celebrate the vision and value the leadership of others, then when our season comes, we will have favor.

Everyone should have the opportunity to be heard. However, it should not be at the expense of a pastor, supervisor, or a parent who has spent sleepless nights building a legacy just to have it destroyed and swept from under his or her feet because of foolish arrogance. No! Walk in your own dominion and do well where you are.

Peter, the bold disciple of Jesus, learned a needed lesson about speaking out of turn: although he meant well, he often spoke with a lack of wisdom. His haste to speak often led to public admonishment. Remember James and John, who asked Jesus if they could sit, one on His right hand and one of His left hand, in glory? One gospel states that even their mother asked Jesus for her sons' promotion. Jesus' immediate response was, "You do not know what you ask. Can you drink from the same cup that I drink from?" (Mark 10:37-40). There is nothing wrong with assertiveness or having a desire for a special seat in the kingdom. However, the question remains, "Are you prepared to handle the level of responsibility that is attached to it?" Be careful of those who will champion your cause before your season. Honor taken is honor not deserved. However, those who labor desire honor; especially considering the cup from which they drink.

Jesus' cup was death, so that His followers could be free from the clutches of Satan. A good leader lives a sacrificial life and excels beyond all barriers. Leaders with insight "value the Peters and appreciate the Judases." These high-spirited men were chosen specifically for Jesus' mission and faced many obstacles with Him.

What motivates you to dream beyond life's barriers? Some teenagers have the mindset that they can do things better than their parents could. They tend to grow up too quickly. I'm sure you remember those days. Yet, we learned that parents, through knowledge and life experiences, should be clear in giving directions. Parental instruction insures that opportunities are not missed, especially those that impart understanding of life's realities in children. It is vitally important to be unambiguous. The fact is that seeds of truth, love, peace, obedience, and steadfastness that grow within us will flourish in due season. Good, bad, or indifferent, if we faithfully nourish good seeds, they will come forth. Our fruit will be revealed (character) and give testimony to who we are.

There is no room for jealousy or envy. These things keep us divided. However, as we build one another up, we are reaching toward greater maturity within ourselves. Improvement in any area of life should be the joy of working together, learning, and benefiting from one another. "In Christ all things have become new" (2 Corinthians 5:17). Our self-esteem and how we react, now that we have the mind of Christ, have changed. There is no need for camouflage! Walk in love. Jesus made it evident that He came to do the will of His Father. He was exalted as Lord, and gave us a name that we can depend upon for our success. Jesus never stepped from under the covering of God's plan and purpose. He made the statement, "If it be possible, let this cup pass from me: nevertheless not as I will, but as thou wilt" (Matthew 26:39, KJV). He knew that His desire was to please God in spite of the suffering He would have to endure. This was love, the greatest of all virtues.

So, why are we so quick to give in and give up? Remember the words of Paul in 1 Corinthians 15:58, KJV: "Therefore, my beloved brethren, be ye steadfast, unmovable, always abounding in the work of the Lord, forasmuch as ye know that your labor is not in vain in the Lord."

Why do we fret? Is it because we look at the successes of others? Could it be the fear of not reaching a goal? It may be the fear of rejection. It could be the lessons we have learned about life and its realities. Whatever it might be, love teaches us to render service with an open heart and a pure conscience without hidden motives or personal agendas. If you can make it past yourself, you will find that the rewards are huge. Ruth served Naomi and walked right into her Boaz. Elisha served Elijah and received a double portion of his anointing. David served Saul, even while dodging and running from spears and javelins. Yet, he persevered, remembering the Word of the Lord. He remembered that Saul was God's king and when he had the opportunity to kill him, he "touched not the anointed and did him no harm" (1 Chronicles 16:22). David's respect for Saul's kingship was because of the fact that it was an ordained position. David continued to serve and by sowing, he reaped enormous benefits when he was crowned king. Saul, on the other hand, could not appreciate David's anointing but decided to kill him because of his own jealousy and anger.

The Bible also says to be careful when one speaks against God's anointed people, as did Miriam about Moses in Numbers 12:1-10, when she was cursed with leprosy. We must watch how we treat those who rule over us. Many will pave the way to our victory, so we must keep in mind that "The eyes of the Lord are in every place, beholding the evil and the good" (Proverbs 15:3, KJV). God honors sincere leadership, but He also honors those that esteem them in love for their works' sake. We do not serve a God who forgets those who labor in love.

We are commanded to love our neighbors as ourselves (Leviticus 19:18, NIV; Matthew 12:31, NIV). We are also reminded that whatever we do to the least of God's people, we have also done it to Jesus and no such act is left unnoticed. Promotion comes from God. Do well always, and be sure to regard the needs of others as being more important than your own.

Paul passed on to Timothy what he expected Timothy to commit to other faithful people. He took Timothy under his wing, teaching him to endure hardship as a good soldier and showing him the ropes. The faithfulness to teach has often drained many leaders, because of personal anxieties, recent misfortunes, or experiences that continue to linger in the present. They find themselves incapable of instructing, and lacking the ability to pass on needed information. Some leaders are torn within, making it hard to trust those around them. This ultimately impedes the covenant of impartation and severs the connection to anything that has the potential to establish a bond that will launch greater developments within the home, workplace, and ministry. Relationships should be constructed so that there is truthfulness and loyalty among those who labor among you.

When writing out the vision or rules of the house, be sure to make your vision clear. Never assume compliance or expect instructions to be followed concisely if your written vision is not clear.

The importance of knowing who labors among you is to identify characteristics that look beyond surface skills to the heart.

As leaders and lay members, we are to edify one another's spirits with truth and encouragement, which strengthen and allow us to build stronger bonds. The purpose is not to establish a buddy-buddy relationship. People become disrespectful sometimes when they become too familiar and take each other for granted, which can be detrimental to all involved. The spirit of familiarity has caused individuals to lose focus and become addicted to other people's emotions, which can be very dangerous.

Since we are known by our fruit, we are to know those who labor among us. We must ask ourselves how well we commune with others. Do we have an open-door policy to discuss ideas? Can we disagree and not be disagreeable? What are the limitations? This is so crucial for leaders of any group of people. Even parents need to understand that children have different personalities and they express themselves accordingly. Do not compare one child to another, but discover the hidden jewels inside each person. Embrace the man or woman who oversees your welfare, who genuinely cares, without comparing that person to other achievers. Jesus looks on the inner person while we focus on the outer person, and often miss life's greatest treasures by doing so. An old saying goes, "We don't miss what we have until it's gone." Why? We are insensitive to those who struggle with us. Perhaps we take for granted those who go the extra mile to complete the task. (Because we fail to applaud, we are not sensitive to those who struggle with us, and do not go the extra mile, seeing a job to its end.) Habakkuk said, "Write the vision, and make it plain so that they may run that read it" (Habakkuk 2:2). It is imperative that we do this. You don't have to know the end results to know whether you are headed in the right direction. For example, wives are often accused of not following their husbands' visions. Yet, there are times when a husband runs off in a direction unknown to the wife.

Sometimes, husbands forget that wives are helpmates. If we expect mature followers, our attitudes must reflect the same. It is our task to know when God is speaking and obey Him. If we fail to obey Him, we could spend years circling our promised land. For the most part, many believers have not trained their ears to hear and know the voice of God. Jesus told His followers to make disciples of men.

Moses knew God's desires and His ways, but the people did not know Moses, God's servant. They hesitated in their walk and many dishonored him. He took upon himself the weight of leading great numbers of people until God instructed him through his father-in-law to appoint elders and officers over the people to assist him in rightly judging the issues at hand and to help him and Aaron lead the people to the land of promise.

God spoke these words to Moses, "I will take of the spirit which is upon you, and will put it upon them; and they shall bear the burden of the people with thee, that thou bear it not thyself alone" (Numbers 11:16-17). Some complained continuously throughout the desert journey, but within the group were two chosen vessels by the names of Joshua and Caleb, who were being developed for leadership. When the time came and they were sent out to spy on the land, these two men brought back a positive report. They believed that they could take the land with God's help. They were courageous and would not back down. They were ready to go forth in the name of the Lord at any cost. God has blessed us with strong individuals and wise people to help us move our visions and the dreams to their destiny.

We read the account of Jesus calling His disciples in Matthew 4:18-22; Mark 1:16-20; and Luke 5:10-11. Jesus chose His staff very carefully. He chose a tax collector, a doctor, and fishermen, to name a few. He looked beyond the outward man and chose men of different character, skill levels, and backgrounds. These were men whom Jesus had to teach, lead, and guide into spiritual maturity. Without a doubt, this was a challenge for all of them, even Jesus. So, what lesson do we learn from Jesus our Lord? Why did He not appoint persons or seek disciples from the popular religious sect of the times? Jesus did then and continues today to pluck those who are teachable from those who are seemingly unlikely. These disciples were men who loved and respected Jesus. Over and over again in our walk, we find full-grown men and women who lack maturity—some wanting to get beyond deeply rooted fears, while some are comfortable with childish behavior.

When stepping into an unfamiliar arena under the authority of another, the strain of humbling oneself becomes very visible. Unless we are willing to humble ourselves, we will never be exalted into the destiny God has for our lives. I admonish parents, leaders, and pastors, as well as children, employees, and church members to know those who labor among you and esteem them highly in love for the sake of their work. Be wise! Receive those of like passion in the Lord with gladness. "...be at peace among yourselves" (1 Thessalonians 5:13, KJV). We carry too much turmoil in our minds. It is time to speak *to* one another and not *at* each other. Obey the Scripture, "Follow peace with all men" (Hebrews 12:14). Move beyond the technicalities of the resume to building relationships—to know someone is having an equal opportunity to spend time with him or her, not making assumptions. If we truly love our neighbors as ourselves, we learn to treat others as we want and expect them to treat us, and this is God's will. Keep in mind that there will be times of rebuke and restraint, but love covers a multitude of faults, and God is our example of true love.

Can you remember a teacher who was demanding, but made a great impact on your life? "Remember the sacrifice of those who made a difference in your life. Consider the outcome of their way of living (lifestyle) and continuously imitate them. "Respect those who work hard among you, who are over you in the Lord and who admonish you. Hold them in the highest regard in love because of their work" (1 Thessalonians 5:12-13, NIV). Don't be afraid to be held accountable — this is a must for all of us. "Live in harmony as well as can be, warn those who are idle, encourage the timid, help the weak, be patient with one and all"(1 Thessalonians 5:14).

Jesus put an end to the concept of "an eye for an eye." This kind of thinking only led to death. He said, "I come to give you life and life more abundantly." In other words, there was no need for payback, because God has promised to avenge us. Seek to be kind and respectful always to those whom you encounter; do not be hasty to judge; it may be that you will entertain angels unawares (see 1 Thessalonians 5:12-16). "Be joyful; pray continually; give thanks in all circumstances, for this is God's will for you in Christ Jesus" (1 Thessalonians 5:16).

A Word of Caution

"Beware of false prophets, who come to you in sheep's clothing, but inwardly they are ravenous wolves" (Matthew 7:15, NASU).

"Do men gather grapes from thorn-bushes or figs from thistles? Even so, every good tree bears good fruit, but a bad tree bears bad fruit. A good tree cannot bear bad fruit, nor can a bad tree bear good fruit. Every tree that does not bear good fruit is cut down and thrown into the fire." (Matthew 7:16-19, NKJV)

"You will know them by their fruits."

(Matthew 7:16)

"Not everyone who says to Me. 'Lord, Lord,' shall enter the kingdom of heaven, but he who does the will of My Father in heaven. Many will say to me in that day, Lord, Lord, have we not prophesied in Your name, cast out demons in Your name, and done many wonders in Your name? And then I will declare to them, I never knew you, depart from me, you who practice lawlessness!'" (Matthew 7:21-23, NKJV).

XXVI THOSE WHO LABOR AMONG US

~CHAPTER ONE~
COMMITMENT

Anything worth having takes commitment. We should be elated in knowing that God valued us enough to give His Son as a sacrifice for humankind. Jesus committed to die for the souls of humankind.

What an assurance we have! There is no wonder or doubt of that dedication. Now that was Jesus, but how are we measuring up to the challenges of life? Ask yourself this question: "Am I willing to obligate myself for the duration of the task?" You are either a good tree with good fruit or a corrupt tree with corrupt fruit. One thing is for sure: you are known by your fruit. We seldom know the ins and outs of day-to-day ventures. For instance, when we are starting a new job, we commit ourselves to being on time, serving to the best of our ability, and working overtime if needed. Aside from that, we have families and complete lists of goals and ideas. The challenge comes when we have to sort and work out life's destiny, a plan

God ordained for each of us. Jeremiah 1:5 and 29:11 both speak to the plans God predestined.

Commitment is a pledge we have decided within ourselves to carry out. Jesus' twelve disciples committed themselves to a man they knew little about. What caught their attention? They too had careers and families, but the Scriptures say that they dropped what they were doing to follow Christ. They were willing to trust—to step out into the unknown.

"With loving-kindness have I drawn thee," said the Lord in Jeremiah 31:3, KJV. True love in the character of an individual will always attract loyalty. Many of you reading this book were abused or abandoned in some way. It could have been your mom or dad, or someone you trusted, who would be there to support and walk with you through life's dilemmas. In spite of the disappointment, I assure you, God has someone to take a positive role in your life, love you, and commit himself/herself unconditionally to your well-being. Be careful not to let bitterness linger in your heart or drive yourself crazy trying to prove something. Jesus paid it all on the cross through His commitment. Settle down, surrender to God, rely on His Word, His course of action, and devote all allegiance to His order and leadership. He cares more about our welfare and the decisions we make day-to-day than anyone else I know, and He will stand with us through it all.

When a man and woman vow to entrust themselves to each other, a wedding celebration follows, but afterward, the marriage (the real work) begins. Because of their pledge, a couple should be able to work out any differences and persevere during hard times. However, their promise to love has to be foundational in sustaining the development of both individuals. They can't afford to be *partially* united. Commitment means *wholeness*.

In the same way in your work situation, be honest with yourself, know your place, and learn your surroundings—get comfortable with the environment, and love what you do. It is impossible to honor and respect those who labor among us when we care little about ourselves and the jobs we are assigned to do. We seek to love with such selfishness—we put "me, myself, and I" first until challenged. Low self-esteem and pity create envy and jealousy, which is a big issue when we lack true commitment to God and with humankind.

Living a committed life is not something done nonchalantly. It involves true devotion and contentment, being completely secure in what you believe. Priorities are put in proper perspective to fulfill God's mandate for the life that has been sketched and ordained through God's plan of salvation, a blueprint of wonder and joy if followed and lived wholeheartedly.

Focus on responsible living. We have an obligation to take care of the business of God. Make full proof of the ministry you are called to do. Remember that all good and perfect gifts come from above, to be used for the glory of God—He who made us. Success comes from knowing that Jesus is the giver and that "It is no longer I ... but Christ who lives in me" declared Paul (Galatians 2:20, RSV). There is no cause to be insecure. No organization of any kind can successfully maintain itself without sincere dedication given from all. A leader must be thoroughly convinced of the task at hand to willingly and patiently convey knowledge to those who labor with him or her in order to substantiate the vision. People are led by example—whether faithful or fearful—a transformation is made—a transfer takes place.

We tend to expect more than what we are willing to give. Think about it. Leaving children unsupervised in hopes that the school system or the Sunday school teachers will effectively teach guarantees that these children will not be "A" students. Where is the foundation? What happened to the cliché, "The family that prays together stays together?" The answer to being committed is about being involved—staying in the race until the end. People rely upon those who lead them. As much as you engage their support, they lean on yours. Their mental state must be purged of the old and processed and renewed in order for any change to take place. Individuals who are committed to the norm will find it difficult to see beyond their circumstances, but God has made a way of escape for those who dare to believe. Commitment will allow you to hold fast to the promise you've made to God and yourself, regardless of who comes or goes, but with an intention to build up and not tear down. Don't get stuck on hurt. Having an understanding of who you are in God will bring persons to your path with talents and gifts to help you build and reach the vision God has declared. The heart of each individual is being conditioned by the desire to see God's best. Even in the secular world, a good employer respects the labor of her or his employees and vice versa. The sweat of those who paved the way for the success of the company's growth is appreciated. Therefore, persons should come with the mindset to add value to the workplace through positive thinking. Do not fool yourself into thinking it is all about talent and skill. Much prayer is recommended. The truth of the matter is that it is not about us or what we can do. Remember, God ordained His plans from the beginning—while we were still in the womb, a plan of prosperity was made for our minds, souls, and bodies to do great things on earth.

Staff, colleagues, and co-workers all are caring people, some with degrees and great accomplishments under their belts, and some, not all, with various gifts, which we respect. However, consider this honor those who are committed to prayer, hard work, and who honestly believe in reaching far beyond the mediocrity of life's dreams. These are they who stick during hard times, when things get wacky, or when others walk out, who can discern change— good, bad, or indifferent.

Commitment comes with a price; not with good intentions. Do not be distracted by heresies. Be aware of flattery, deceitfulness, and backbiting without participating. Remember that those who labor among you are there either for your good to build up and see the completion of the vision, or to do evil, take from, and destroy, not just the work but also the reputation that has been built. Commitment does not stand alone, but upon a foundation of truth—God's truth. We must believe we can do all things through Christ, not ourselves, and commit to Him wholeheartedly. Welcome His presence with thanksgiving— He can do what we cannot, and without doubt, walk in the assurance that it is done by faith.

No family, business, or ministry can be successful outside of God's grace, whether we admit that or not. Do what you purpose in your heart, regardless of circumstances. There will always be opportunities to achieve great accomplishments, some not as easy as others, but all with use of various gifts, which we respect. However, consider this honor: those who are committed to prayer, hard work, and who honestly believe in reaching far beyond the mediocrity of life's dreams. These are those who stick during hard times, when things get wacky, or others walk out, and who can discern change— good, bad, or indifferent.

There will always be hurdles to leap over. If someone walks away, let that person go. If he or she is disruptive, have this person sit down and talk to him or her. He or she will find out the reality of life, and you will have helped him or her.

Commitment calls for hard work, long hours, and very few pats on the back. Devoted people are blessed, prosperous, and refined; they have pledged to serve to the best of their ability and to commit themselves to the cause. When we verbally agree to do something, it means nothing if we do not follow through. The agreement is not fulfilled until the task is finished. It is easy to make a pledge, but good intentions get us nowhere fast. We should be bound, not just to a house, but to a home; not just to an average church, but to a soul-winning, life-changing, Bible-believing church.

Remember, the workplace will prosper where there is sincere commitment. The heart of each individual is being conditioned by the desire to see one's best. A good worker respects the labor of his or her co-workers, yet we seem to have lost the desire to respect or simply show consideration for one another. Jesus declared that this day would come; He said, "Because iniquity shall abound, the love of many shall wax cold" (Matthew 24:12, KJV), and this is evident in some of our churches.

~CHAPTER TWO~

TRUSTWORTHINESS

Trust is a vital component in any relationship. Yet, I do not know of anyone who has not been betrayed at one time or another by someone whom they have trusted. Jesus is the perfect example of that. Living a creditable lifestyle as leaders and laypersons is a mandate that only responsible people will even attempt to manage. It takes self-discipline to be trustworthy, a characteristic we should all desire. Make sure there is someone to whom you are held accountable. Learn to hold on to those things that have been placed in your heart until it is time to release them. We all should evaluate ourselves by asking the question: Can I be trusted? Am I reliable? What is the weight of my integrity? The Word of God says to judge yourself that you be not judged (see Matthew 7:1). Put yourself under the microscope rather than highlighting the wrong in a brother or sister or avoiding your own faults, and pay attention to what you are truly capable of doing. "Gossip betrays a confidence, but a trustworthy man keeps a secret" (Proverbs 11:13, NIV).

"Who can I confide in?" Is this not the question we all ask, desiring true friendship?

James wanted to know if a fountain could bring forth sweet and bitter water at the same time (James 3:11), or, as we would say, it is wrong to "talk out of both sides of the mouth." No person who talks too much or who does not listen is one with whom we want to share our ideas. There is nothing worse than a nosy pest, spilling gossip everywhere. Whether things are shared in the boardroom or the bedroom, our inner thoughts or ideas are private—not to be broadcast to all and sundry. Our parents had a saying that went, "Whatever goes on in this house stays in this house." Telling your best friend a secret or something you should not share may cost you your marriage, your ministry, or be the reason your business fails, especially when there is no genuine trust or perhaps the person with whom you are conversing does not have your best interests at heart.

Trust is the bond that creates success, births businesses, builds strong family structures, and brings great ministries into reality. Confidentiality is one of the keys to trust. When you break faith or release information without permission, you close the door to trust and opportunities for yourself. Never think you are getting over just because a situation is not addressed immediately. Jesus was always conscious of those around Him; He knew their hearts and taught them how to be wise. Within His circle of friends, even the one chosen to betray Him, Jesus was not deceptive. Know your boundaries with others. Watch the one who sits with you with nothing to say. This person may absorb information, but for whom? If someone keeps up with your itinerary but never shows up to support your visions, this should be a red flag. Don't get bitten by the kiss of betrayal! It is our responsibility to watch and pray, lest we are led into temptation. You cannot divulge secrets or confidential information to a person without knowing his or her convictions.

Paul wrote in 1 Timothy 1:12: "I thank Christ Jesus our Lord, who has strengthened me; because He considered me faithful, putting me into service." Think about that. There is no greater honor than to be chosen because one is considered faithful and reliable before God and humankind. This is not talking about someone who is waiting on a promotion, but one who is positioned to be promoted based upon character, integrity, and performance. Some people work hard, but their dispositions stink. They can only see and point out the negative;

they are very timely, even most dependable, but not always honest. Give this some thought. Are you worthy of the trust and the accolades given you? Have you earned that respect, attention, and pat on the back that is so seemingly needed in order to be affirmed, or can your reliable nature speak for you?

As leaders, we are responsible for many things and wear many hats, but that says nothing if we are not trustworthy. Our society is filled with busy people—those who are busy lying, stealing, procrastinating, and deceiving, which Jesus predicted would happen. God has an expectation that we will fulfill our responsibilities by being imitators of Him. Hold on to the vision. Don't be negligent, creating greater problems; be the problem solver. If someone entrusts you to carry out an assignment and you drop the ball, this creates hardship for someone else and causes your brothers or sisters, mainly those in leadership, to carry an extra load. If you do not know and find yourself in a struggle, stop. Seek help, but don't just throw up your hands. Do you think that successful businesses and ministries would have lasted if individuals folded their arms because someone felt like giving up and throwing in the towel? We put too much confidence in people rather than God. Remember this Scripture, Proverbs 3:5-6, that reads: "Trust in the Lord with all your heart and lean not on your own understanding: In all your ways acknowledge Him, and He shall direct your pathway." When given a job to do, do it! Rely upon the wisdom of God to help you and do not deviate.

God's purpose will be manifest in and through us as we yield to the assignments given us as people with revelation, hope, and dreams. The Scriptures say: "Being confident of this very thing, that he which has begun a good work in you will perform or complete it until the day of Jesus Christ" (Philippians 1:6). We are charged to fulfill and wholeheartedly carry out all responsibilities and obligations. "Out of the same mouth proceed blessings and cursing. My brothers, these things ought not to be" (James 3:10). Be astute, endued with knowledge, speak out of good conversation with meekness of wisdom Let your fruit of trustworthiness be accepted by the Lord. We spend much of our time trying to please humans when in fact if we please God and He is satisfied, no one else will have to wonder whether we are doing the right thing. God is our judge; He beholds the good and evil of humanity and will recompense accordingly.

~CHAPTER THREE~

FAITHFULNESS

You will know them by their fruits.

(Matthew 7:16, NKJV)

I am devoted to that which I believe to be the true meaning of being faithful. Paul said in Colossians, "I'm sending my beloved brother, a faithful minister, and fellow servant, who will tell you all the news about me. Sending him for this purpose, that he may know your circumstances and comfort your hearts, along with another faithful brother, they will make known to you what is happening." The responsibility of having a vision implanted in our hearts is to impart unto those laboring among us, to be assured that the message sent will reach its hearers and be accurate. Every detail must be engineered, which is passed down and put into motion by those authentic ones who are without hidden agendas a product and representation of the employer, pastor, and or parent, who surrenders and submits to the call of God.

It is impossible to sincerely support anything that does not conform to your beliefs. Sooner or later, you will walk away drained and miserable as you try to please people. Instead, be prudent; put every effort to being all about kingdom building with purpose and following the direction of the Holy Ghost. Since faith is the substance of things hoped for, (things believed in) and the evidence or manifestation of things not seen, this means that individuals should be able to move forward without agonizing over unrealized material expectations. Therefore, these individuals understand the level of integrity and spirit of excellence. It is essential to be full of faith, resolving all doubt and spirits of hindrance. The end results will not be revealed when starting a project, ministry, or business, but the level of faith should reside in the heart until completion. God is faithful in all things. He is not slack concerning His promises towards us. The persons you supervise, your followers, can produce no more than that which you devote yourself to do. If you procrastinate, so will they. Do not expect others to produce your dream. You are the visionary, while they may only be there for a season. Though the vision may tarry it is for an appointed time (Habakkuk 2:3). Be persistent and prepared; give ear to instruction. If you acknowledge God, God will direct your path.

We cannot afford to miss God's divine timing. It must be respected. Our futures and the fate of others rely on it. When given the green light to move ahead, it is unknown to us whether or not one's destiny will be to become the next president or allow one to receive or discover the antidote for an incurable disease.

Understand that we are not waiting just to step into God's perfect plan. He has given us power (to tread over serpents; to walk in authority; and to proclaim the acceptable year of the Lord), love (what greater love than to give for the sake of a friend), and sound minds (we have more than enough double-minded, undependable people in our workplaces and churches; God is calling for people with stable minds (see 2 Timothy 1:7; James 1:8).

God has shown us through our forefathers that we can "possess the land." Keep in mind, though you may have a staff of ten, twelve, etc., that not everyone will see what you see or have the faith to do what you ask of him or her. Do not fear or be disturbed: faith in God assures us of His presence. Some may not catch the vision immediately, but are committed to loving and respecting you as a person. Jesus' disciples did not comprehend many things, but given the times, Jesus was able to communicate with them about things others could not digest. With all the instructions He gave, Jesus chose men who were sensitive to divine revelation and who walked closely with Him. Peter, James, and John were disciples He kept even closer by imparting information that allowed them to experience great interventions in the spirit, which prepared them for the awesome call upon their lives.

The disciples came to the point of doing what was required of them, but they trusted in the One who led them. In other words, everyone has a place, some jobs are more demanding than others, but never underestimate the little Davids, Timothys, the elderly Sarahs who birthed nations, or the Esthers who will go before kings on behalf of the people, knowing that they may not be received well by others, but having the assurance that God is with them, and failure is not an option.

Be an example of what you teach—be an effective communicator. Can you lead a nation to victory, as the anointed prophetess Deborah did, or like Abraham, who stepped into the unknown with a promise that was fulfilled in his latter days. Think about the little maid who spoke to Naaman, captain of the army, who believed in her God and the prophet Elijah. Which one of your family members, board members, or staff persons will catch your mantle and give support to your vision? Are you faithful in believing God for the desires in your heart as you want others to be to you? Faith gives us favor when all odds are against us, and it will turn the table for us when molehills look like mountains, and the enemy is raging against us. The faithful are kingdom warriors, ready to face unwelcome obstacles. Faith moves God—not tears of sympathy or the act of feeling sorry for oneself.

God is the repairer of the breach, bridging lives through reconciliation and canceling debts where our wrong decisions have caused our finances to dwindle. He favors us and covers bad credit when it seems beyond restoring. Be careful how you serve others on your way up—they may be the people who will in turn serve you. Whether faithful or faithless, we set an example. Faith is not just confession of words, but the way those words are put into action. It is moving out on nothing, believing something is there. Being faithful to our faith enables us to accomplish all things. We are skilled to do God's will and purpose because we believe we can do this as faithful followers. God said that those who are faithful would prosper in what they do! Faith comes by hearing ("I can do all things through Christ who strengthens me"—Philippians 4:13, NKJV, for example.) Live as an example of your teaching while walking in the Word in full assurance of your ability in God. Faithfulness is obedience to God's full command when trials of the flesh are bearing down on you.

How badly do you want to be successful? I am talking about true success, without regret, shame, or guilt. What is it worth to you? Whatever you sow, you reap, without condemnation.

When faith is limited, we shortchange ourselves and those who follow us. God gave each of us not only a measure of faith, but also the tools to mature in it. The people you serve symbolize principle, image, and thoughts. They trust that you are responsible in hearing from God, and that you have their best interests at heart to endure in good times and in not-so-good times.

David spoke to Saul in 1 Samuel 26:23, NIV: "The Lord rewards every man for his righteousness and faithfulness. The LORD delivered you into my hands today, but I would not lay a hand on the Lord's anointed." Would it have been self-defense for David to retaliate against Saul? Certainly it would have been, but David pushed beyond what his worldly desires demanded for him to do.

Be conscious of the fact that God is our judge and He watches over our faithful deeds. He is the One whom we want to please. Even when situations seem to be against us, we must remain faithful. It is in times like this that many people start to think they can outdo God. They may say, "I can take it from here, God." However, this is the very time when we should denounce pride and tell ourselves that God rewards those who diligently (meticulously, carefully) seek His way, and He is focused on carrying out His purpose and what He wants our destiny to be.

~CHAPTER FOUR~

OBEDIENCE

You will know them by their fruits.

(Matthew 7:16)

Obedience is better than any sacrifice if you want true peace. It seems that we are willing to sacrifice our time, money, and even our loved ones rather than simply obey God's Word. "Everyone has heard about your obedience, so I am full of joy over you, but I want you to be wise about what is good, and innocent about what is evil" (Romans 16:19, NIV). People are always ready to pay their way out, but God delights in our eagerness to obey Him, not in what or how much we can give Him by showing up on Sunday morning. While such devotion is great, we may struggle the night prior to following through with it. Monday through Friday, we wrestle with obedience. Our flesh rejects it, and we pout at any rebuke or instruction from authority, not truly realizing that life is as a vapor. People, themselves, would rather give material things than to repent, be humbled, or apologize for wrongdoing. God is not after what we can give; our sacrifices mean nothing if they are not done in faith and obedience. Without faith, the Bible declares that it is impossible to please God. So we limit the fullness of what God chooses to do in our lives through grumbling, complaining, and in-your-face defiance.

Believing by faith that God is Lord enables us to walk in obedience and reach heights beyond our imagination. Whatever possessions we may have do not make us blessed people. True blessings come through doing what God commands, regardless of the circumstances. For instance, Joseph is an example of a man who went from abandonment, betrayal, and incarceration to the royal palace, yet in all phases of his life he remained faithful.

Can you submit to God wholeheartedly? Cain found this so hard that he killed his brother. Scripture lets us know that the heart is desperately wicked. Who knows the heart today? Cain is still known, even today, by the evil fruit of his heart. There are so many lessons before us of those who refused to obey God and were punished—yet, we continue to act like our own outcomes will be different. We must surrender to God's way. He is the great "I AM"!

Obedience means completeness (see Joshua 11:15). "As the LORD commanded Moses his servant, so did Moses command Joshua, and so did Joshua: he left nothing undone of all that the Lord commanded." As leaders, we are called on and chosen to complete tasks as well as follow directions. Regardless of what we may think or feel, this is a mandate, and we were created for God's purposes. So, we must stop trying to change the plan ordained for life. Be loyal followers with unwavering dedication to hard work and earned promotions. Our ways may seem right, but may not be right according to God's plans. This kind of thinking can often lead us to a wedge that separates us from God's love. Be watchful of the actions you communicate in your lifestyle and conversation, and careful that your words do not become strong against the Lord. Obey God at all costs. Sincere laborers will always keep in step, looking to learn from those ahead of them. Why work with friction and constant complaining? Learn how to obey, especially when opposition confronts you and society's pressure overwhelms you. Your ideas may be better, but if you were not given the vision, just comply with the visionary. Ask when in doubt, and be willing to submit. The word *obedience* is not to belittle you. No, my friend, just the opposite—obedience exemplifies moral fiber.

~CHAPTER FIVE~
LOYALTY

Persistent giving of oneself, no matter the sacrifice, indicates loyalty, and this kind of person is one with whom you can share your heart without fear of treachery. It indicates a high level of respect when things are good, bad, or indifferent; it is the reason that we see more loyalty in gangs and wicked arenas than we do in respectable places, such as churches and creditable businesses. If our allegiance is to the Lord as believers, we are sold out to do His will, so submitting to authority should not be a struggle. When both the leader and staff persons have the mindset of excellence and their intention is to please God more than themselves, there will be a spirit of devotion towards one other and the vision will be successful. In this kind of situation, everyone is held accountable, everyone considers each other's goals and objectives, and working together becomes constant and pleasant in the workplace.

Be willing to serve and defend your cause. A person who is loyal does not have to be sought out—he or she is reliable, always in place, and ready to respond to the call of command, even when it means going against the grain. The appreciation of loyalty and truth will follow in the days to come. Our government would not be in the shape it is in if only people were loyal, trusted individuals. The church hurts for the lack of dependability in leadership and membership. Is there devotion to anything today? People are not stable; they are very unpredictable. Where do they go? They may be hopping and skipping from place to place—and if you try to keep up with them, all your standards will be diminished as well. So I caution you to not be hasty in having a lot of voices around you. Seek sound doctrine and counseling from proven individuals. Everyone has an opinion, and if we are not careful, the spirit of manipulation will become overpowering.

Just as the disciples could not understand Jesus' mysteries, neither can you articulate every issue that may arise. Be wise—not everyone is loyal to God or to you, so be mindful of this in a relationship and your commitment to others. Be sober and alert in business, having a watchful eye. The expression, "It is what it is" can apply here. Don't be blind, even in friendship. Loyalty comes from a sincere heart, allowing your faithfulness, trustworthiness, and commitment to lighten the load and brighten the road for others who dare to tread the pathway. A word to the wise: a loyal companion is hard to find, but worth the trouble of finding him or her.

~Chapter Six~
CONCLUSION

Getting to know those around you could be a true life saver. Be open minded to new ideas and observe the potential in others while building an effective group of committed, trustworthy, loyal, faithful, and obedient laborers. Finding such a person of integrity may possibly mean that you've found a true friend. The most valuable lesson that I have obtained is taken from James 1:19: "Be swift to listen, slow to speak," especially when you believe you are right. Paul wrote, "All things are legitimate (permissible, and we are free to do anything we please), but not all things are helpful, expedient, profitable, or wholesome, nor does it edify" (1 Corinthians 10:23). God has also impressed upon me this truth: "I said, I will take heed and guard my ways that I sin not with my tongue" (Psalm 39:1).

I pray that this book is a blessing to you. It is my hope that it will be a thoughtful source when faced with decisions at work, at home, and in ministry. Pray for direction, seek God's counsel, and reach the level of excellence God has ordained for you. Remember: God exalts one who humbles himself, but he that exalts himself God will bring down. He opens doors no human can shut, and closes doors that no one can open. "Pray without ceasing" (1 Thessalonians 5:17, KJV).

Scripture References KJV, NIV:

Proverbs 16:3; 14:5;

Psalms 4:3; 31:23; 37:5, 119:30

John 15:13

Ephesians 5:1-2; 6:5-9

1 John 3:14-19

Luke 16:10

1 Corinthians 4:2; 16:18

Philippians 2:29

Hebrews 5:8-9; 13:7; 13:17

2 Corinthians 10:5-6

www.ingramcontent.com/pod-product-compliance
Lightning Source LLC
Chambersburg PA
CBHW050607300426
44112CB00013B/2116